D0602962

If You Were a
Chocolate Mustache

If You Were a Chocolate Mustache

Poems by Children's Poet Laureate J. Patrick Lewis

Drawings by Matthew Cordell

WORDSONG

HONESDALE, PENNSYLVANIA

If You Were a Chocolate Mustache
Poems by J. Patrick Lewis
Drawings by Matthew Cordell

Text copyright © 2012 by J. Patrick Lewis
Drawings copyright © 2012 by Matthew Cordell

"The Bog Poet" was first published in the August 2008 issue of *Cricket* magazine.
"Honk If You're a Reader" was first published in the July 2009 issue of *Language Arts*.
"Nicknames in the NBA" was first published in the anthology *The Arrow Finds Its Mark: A Book of Found Poems*, edited by
  Georgia Heard, copyright © 2012, Roaring Brook Press.
"Papa Bear" was first published in the anthology *Poems for Fathers*, selected by Myra Cohn Livingston, copyright © 1989,
  Holiday House; it later appeared in the anthology *Ring Out Wild Bells*, selected by Lee Bennett Hopkins, copyright © 1992,
  Harcourt Brace.
"Spoiled Rotten" was first published in the anthology *Nasty Bugs*, selected by Lee Bennett Hopkins, copyright © 2012, Dial.

On page 121, the poem "The Universal Turtle Verse" and accompanying artwork are an homage to the famous children's poet
  Shel Silverstein and his wonderful poems and books, but they imply no endorsement or authorization by Mr. Silverstein or
  his heirs or estate.

WORDʃONG
An Imprint of Boyds Mills Press, Inc.
815 Church Street
Honesdale, Pennsylvania 18431
Printed in the United States of America

ISBN: 978-1-59078-927-8
Library of Congress Control Number: 2012939794

First edition
10 9 8 7 6 5 4 3 2 1

Design by Barbara Grzeslo
Production by Margaret Mosomillo
The text for this book is set in Candida
The drawings are done in pen and ink.

For Sue
—JPL

For Julie and Romy
—MC

The Backward Man

There was a man from Santa Cruz
Who sold his shiny Sunday shoes—
The shoelaces,
The shoelace holes,
The heels and tongues.
He sold the soles.
And not one thing was overlooked—
He sold the steps the shoes once took!

The nincompoop who bought the shoes
Now walks around in Santa Cruz
But always with a backward look,
Taking steps the shoes once took.

One Lost Sock

Quandary?
Laundry.
Try yer
Dryer.

Dragon Dryer

Sitting in the corner
Is a Dragon in a crate.

I push its belly button,
Then I watch it agitate
Heavy Duty/Cottons/
Linens/Delicates . . .
                    Wham!
It thumps against the Washer
Monster—*blam, blam, blam!*
The Dragon Dryer's rocking
On its heels and toes
So hard I think it must be
Having breakfast, *Toastie Clothes.*
Finally, I think it's safe
To creep up on the beast.
Dragon D. enjoyed himself:
The laundry is deceased!

Bear One, Bear Two

Bear One was big, Bear Two, look-see!
They tipped the scales at GET OFF ME!
Bear One got thin, like Two, his twin—
A double loss of a triple chin.

Bear One got sick—what a dirty trick.
Bear Two took care of his twin sidekick.
Bear Two told jokes; Bear One got well.
Bear Two said, *"Laughter's a magic spell."*

Bear One said, *"I'm staying home from school,"*
Bear Two said, *"One, that's against the rule."*
Bear One sang a song to a banjo string,
Bear Two sang along to an onion ring.

Bear Two ran away, Bear One stayed home—
Bear Two had the wandering chromosome.
Bear One, sad sack, till Two came back—
A double yolk is hard to crack.

Mexican Jumping Bean

Why does the Mexican jumping bean jump?
Inside the bean, there's a larva-size lump.
The lump was an egg of the bean moth, and now
The caterpillar bean moth is taking a bow
And doing the mambo, the tango . . . *olé!*
(The heat from your hand makes it rock and *rollé!*)

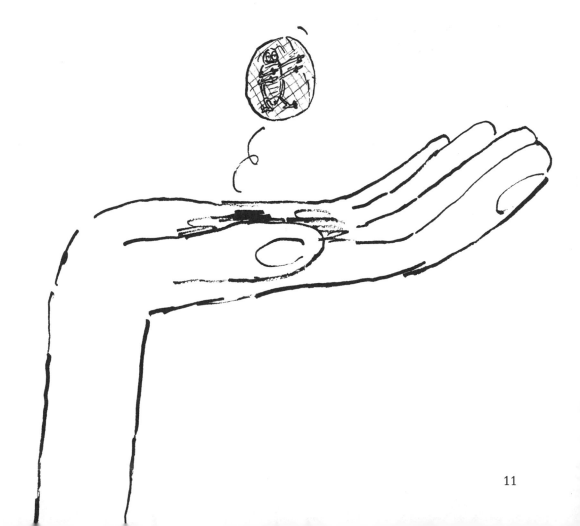

The Longest Watermelon Seed Spit

Lee did the watermelon deed that I think I can super-seed.

Lee Wheelis
68 ft. 9 1/8 in.
Luling, Texas
1989

13

Book Riddles: Three Poems

A Princess naps a hundred years
Until some lippy guy appears.

Sleeping Beauty
Charles Perrault

This tale

b
  e
    c
      o
        m
          e
            s
               a
              t
             r
              a
                i
                l
                    o
                    f
                      c
                        r
                        u
                        m
                        b
                       s
                      .

The Brothers Grimm,
Hansel and Gretel

Exterminator catches pests;
the town refuses his requests.
He sets out to right the wrong
by playing on his flute a song
exciting and inviting . . . that's
when kids start disappearing. *Rats!*

Robert Browning,
The Brothers Grimm,
The Pied Piper of Hamelin

15

Mr. Twisty

I touch my ankle to my shoulder,
And bring my heel up to my waist,
Then curl my leg around my collar
Quite easily although red-faced.
I pinch my shoulder blades together.
My tibia brushes my nose,
My chin caresses my patella.
And Pretzel-Wear's my brand of clothes.

Never Eat Your Pretzels Straight

Oh, never eat your pretzels straight.
A pretzel ought to circul8!
A pretzel fried without a twist
Is like a knuckleball . . . you missed!
A pretzel made without a weave
Is only pretzel make-believe.
A pretzel that's not baked to bend
Deserves the name "Pretzel Pretend,"
"Salt-on-a-Twig," or "Feed the Squirrel."
Pretzels zing when pretzels curl.

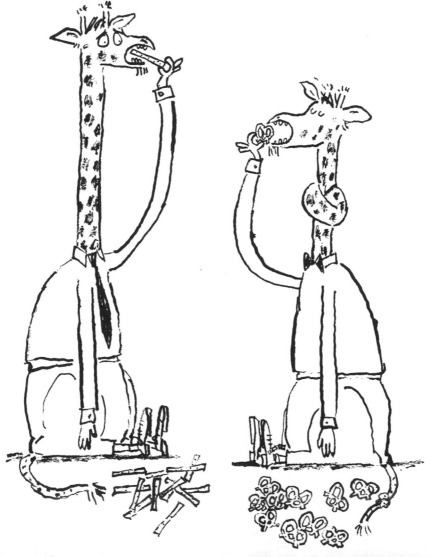

Black & White

A voyage to Antarctica
    Allowed me to pursue
A study of the penguin's ways
    And why he never flew.
"You must admit," the Penguin said,
    "The study's overdue.

"This flipper flips, that flapper flaps—
    You needn't take a note."
(Which would have been impossible;
    The Penguin rocked the boat.)
And while he sharpened icicles,
    He told this anecdote.

"Ducks and geese fly north!" said he.
    "It simply isn't right!
Their overcoats are blue and green,
    They're guaranteed for flight.
We penguins can't get off the ground,
    We're only black and white!"

A better explanation I
    Agreed I never heard.
Surprising, too, it was because
    I'd heard it from a bird.
The Penguin poked his pocket watch
    And left without a word.

Danny Dooley

Danny Dooley, what a dilly,
Danny Dooley, he was swell.
Danny Dooley loved his honey,
Judy Jingle. She's a belle.

Danny Dooley lost his honey,
Lost his true love down a well.
Judy Jingle lost her doozie,
Danny Dooley, when she fell.

Danny Dooley went in mourning
To the well where she fell in.
As he sniffled in his hankie,
So did Judy Jingle's twin.

Danny Dooley fell in love with
Joanie Jingle. She's a peach.
Oh, he still loves *Judy* Jingle,
But she's slightly out of reach.

Hello?...

Never Spit from a Roller Coaster

Whenever you ride a roller coaster,
You should never spit
Unless you are the only person
You intend to hit.

The Bog Poet

I am a working toad.
I keep a log.
I write to keep
From sinking in a bog.
I never show my poems
To other toads
Who write much better lines
And deeper odes
Than I could ever write,
But that's okay.
I'm searching for one
Great Bog Thing to say.

I Knew a Little Kid

I knew a little kid
Who built a pyramid—
Dirty clothes in the middle of his bedroom.
And when he was sleepy,
He slept on his tepee,
But didn't have very much headroom.

23

Travelin' Gal
Real Town Names

We moved away to Finger, Tenn.
  Left so Dull, OH, for good.
My sister lives in small Gas, Kans.,
  A red-hot neighborhood.

Ma said, "How 'bout Hot Coffee, Miss.,
  Or maybe Toast, NC?"
But we leaped over Toad Hop, IN,
  Clear up to Bald Head, ME.

I said, "Let's get a Sandwich, MA."
  "That sounds Delightful, OH.
Do you have any Money, Miss.?"
  "I've got two dimes, Not, MO."

Then we swung down to Carefree, AZ,
  The Ariz. hot and dry.
I wish Ma'd said, "Goodnight, OK."
  But we're in Big Hole, WY?

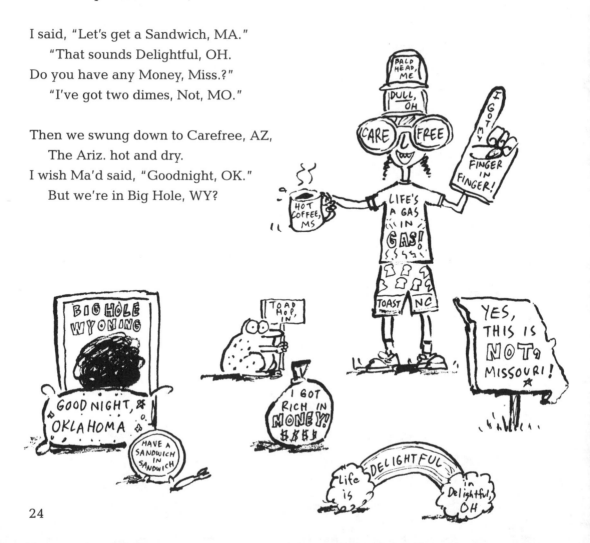

Stuff

I went to a garage sale,
Came home with a garage.
I purchased in the desert
A shimmering mirage.
I bought a secret time machine,
Now I can buy some time.
I took a trip to Scotland Yard
And bought a case of crime.
I almost bought a mirror but
I stopped upon reflection.
I added buggy uncle Al
To my big aunt collection.
I flew a mammoth jet, that's how
I learned to dino-soar.
I practiced my canoeing
And kayaking, either/oar.
I only bought a wildebeest
To meet somebody gnu.
Today I'll rent a U-Haul
And find someone like U.

Hard Times

Peggy Hard
   Wakes at eight,
      Always gets
         To school—late.

Sees a friend,
   Stops to share
      Gossip, gabs,
         Doesn't care.

Peggy meets
   Mrs. Hume,
      Gets a "Tardy—
         Homeroom,"

As her friend,
   Buddy Doyle,
      Watches Peggy
         Hard boil.

School Buses

The yellow hippopotabuses
Raise one red ear
When they are stopping
To tell all drivers
What the fuss is:
Hippopotabus is dropping

Off one last kid, and there's his mother!
Its ear folds up,
Its door is closing.
It knows it's time
To join the other
Hippopotabuses, dozing.

The Animals at the Police Station

The Detectives are detecting,
The Inspectors are inspecting,
When I pull into the station house at noon.
"Sergeant Katz and Captain Chita—
Boys," I say, "I'm gonna need a
Jungle rap sheet to identify each goon."

"Hello, Rockefeller Rhino."
I nod to the rare albino,
Who's got diamond earrings dangling from his horn.
April Ape and Big Kahuna,
Two baboons, are tossing tuna,
While the Lion feeds the Camel caramel corn.

Sly the Weasel, I should mention,
Tries to get the Pig's attention,
But the Pig plays tiddly-winkum with the Bear,
Who is singing to a shady
Undercover agent lady
Hippopotamus with ribbons in her hair.

She is stumped on a crossword puzzle
And she sneezles through her muzzle,
"What's MENAGERIE—three letters. Any clue?"
So to keep from going loco,
I gulp down two cups of cocoa,
And I yell, "Just look around you. It's a ZOO!"

The Moth

Can never be accused of sloth.
She redesigns a tablecloth
Or ventilates a comfy quilt
For which her mouth was specially built.
After the moth is satisfied,
It's most convenient to hide
Her musty coat and dusty wings
In drawers full of your underthings.

At Your Service

Waiters
Serve
Taters,
But
Waders
Serve
Gators.

Spoiled Rotten

I'm a maggot, I'm a marvel
Of the larval generation.
I'm a comma in a drama
Of disgusting devastation.
Multiply me!—I'm a slimy
Bug who's earned his reputation
As I've gotten spoiled rotten.
Want to see a demonstration?

The King of Glue

The King of Glue
Announced a new
Sweet substitute for pie—
A plate of paste
That had the taste
Of stickum—Thick 'n' Dry.

The Prince of Glue
(King Number 2)
Said, "Pie is just the thing
To show the mob
Your royal job,
And prove why you are king."

The Queen of Glue
Said, "Look at who
Would love some Thick 'n' Dry."
For there at dawn
The mob banged on
The gates for pasty pie.

But Mobs of Glue
Could barely chew
Through stickum, thick or thin.
"The king can't cook!"
They cried, and took
Away his rolling pin.

Epigraham Crackers: Four Poems

I think that I shall never chew
Tofu as tasty as a shoe.

The British should apologize
For even *thinking* mincemeat pies.

Long ago, starving, with nothing to eat,
A raving mad man laid his lips on a . . . **beet!**

Animal crackers every kid adores,
But only graham crackers make s'mores.

The Opposite Boy

He sat down lengthwise as he knelt
Upon the ceiling where he hung
Right side up. From there he swung
Motionless until he felt

Night falling from the rising sun.
He went to bath and took a bed.
That's when his mother Henry said,
"Butter a book and read a bun."

He fell awake and sprang asleep.
"Tonight's the day I start to quit
To do the same thing opposite!"
(Which was extremely shallowdeep.)

"I always tell the truth to lie.
Good-bye, hello. Hello, good-bye."

Road Blocks

I saw a bookworm in a book.
The bookworm said to me,
"Long have I lived these many years
On page 6, paragraph 3.

"The author left a blooper trail:
A golfer with a **tea**?
What cat's got **fir**?
What dog's got **hare**?
Have you seen babies **pea**?"

I said, "Why don't you move along?
The best is still ahead."
"The author misspelled **its** for **it's**!
That's where I stopped," she said.

A Human Interviews a Mouse Lemur

What's best about your goggle eyes? *Size.*
What is your greatest body part? *Heart.*
At night, what keeps you wide awake? *Snake.*
Do you prefer leaves, worms, or slugs? *Bugs.*
What beast would scare you at a zoo? *You.*
Where would you like to be at dawn? *Gone.*

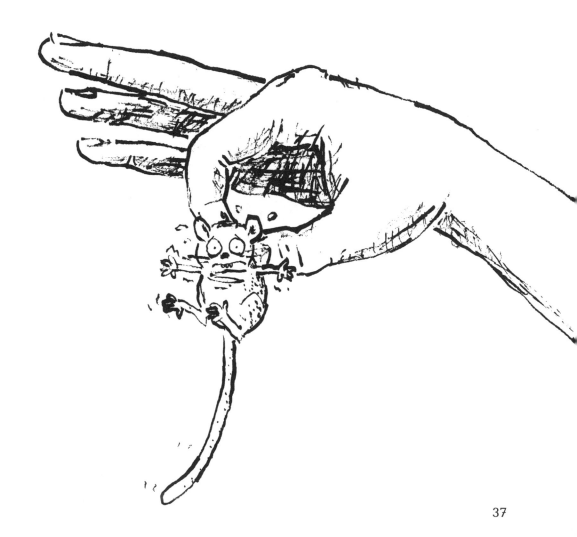

Beaver Babble

Whack us a willow,
Bite us a birch,
Bust us a maple,
Build us a perch.

Tails be wicked,
Teeth be buck,
Timber, honey!
Tree? Tough luck.

Pearly Chompers,
Nibble, gnaw.
Stay sharp, Stumpy.
Sweeeeet, Hacksaw.

Dam us a river,
Plug us a stream,
Weave us a beaver
Beam dream, team.

Kdid

Said Uncle Vlad,
"There's a *Kdid*."
"What's a *Kdid*?"
I said.

"A bad bug word
for a katydid.
Be careful, kid.

"A *Kdid Kdad* can get
as mad as a dragon,"
whispered Uncle Vlad.

He went inside.
I couldn't help it,
I yelled, ***"KDID!
KDID! KDID!"***

(Then I hid!)

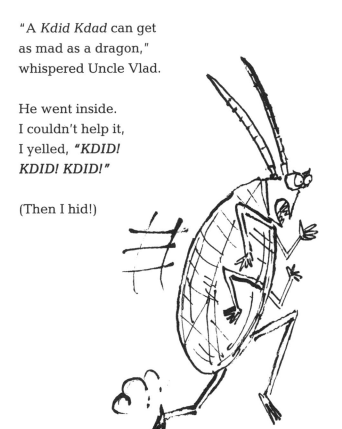

Rules for Tightrope Walking Between Tall Buildings

1. Whatever you do, don't laugh.
2. Avoid looking down at the traf—

Valentine Verses: Four Poems

I wish I were a pistachio
And you were a plump cashew.
Think of all the chocolate bars
Where nutters rendezvous.

Hey there, Paco,
You're for me!
Ginger's nacho
Cup o' tea.

Everyone is dazzled by your

Untie the bow, undo the ribbon,
Open the box, remove the wrap.
If you get lost on the way to my heart,
Here's a flashlight and treasure map.

Anti-Valentine Verses: Four Poems

Benjamin, Benjamin,
What do you think?
I LOVE YOU!
(It's invisible ink.)

When I feel like a cherry,
And you're my cherry pit,
I get so annoyed with you,
I'm mad enough to spit.

Put your hand on my shirt.
Feel something, Penny?
Used to be heartbeats,
Now there aren't any.
I gave them to you
Last Valentine's Day.
That turned out to be
A dead giveaway.

She told me I would be the one
Till buoys were lost at sea,
But when we got to 5th grade,
Her buoyfriend wasn't me.

44

One of a Kind

An old turtle looked up and said,
"Mr. Sky, I have lived a long time.
I have seen it all,
And what they say is true.
There is nothing new under the sun."

"Really?" said Sky.
And from six miles up, he dropped
A single snowflake.

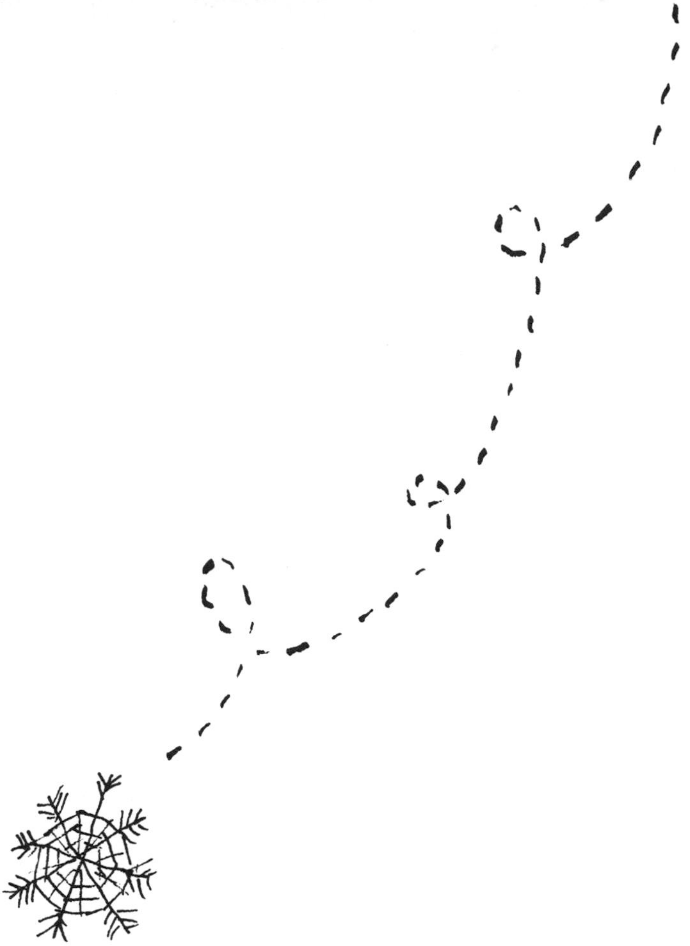

How Big?

You were a kid, I was your pup.
I got bigger as you grew up.
When you were four, I was just two.
I was twice as tall as you.
Now you are twelve, and I am ten.
I weigh more than you do, Ben.
You are my owner, but I am in charge.
You are my captain, I am your barge.
You are a prince, but I am the king.
I am the boss of everything.
You're the conductor, but I am the train.
You're a great kid, and I'm a Great Dane!

Dragon vs. Girl

A Dragon cried, "Help, Mom, that girl
Shot me with her squirt gun!"
The Mother Dragon smiled.
"It's time you had a little fun."

"But Mom . . ."

"Don't 'But Mom' me," she said.
"You've got a flame to throw.
You're spitting *fire*, for blazing's sake.
She's spitting H_2O!"

The battle raged as burning flames
Shot from the Dragon's snout.
The Dragon lost. The squirt gun girl
Had hosed his fire out.

49

More Book Riddles: **Three Poems**

Once a *choo-choo-su-per-man*
pulled a freight train caravan
with four words—*think, I, I, can.*

The Little Engine That Could
Watty Piper

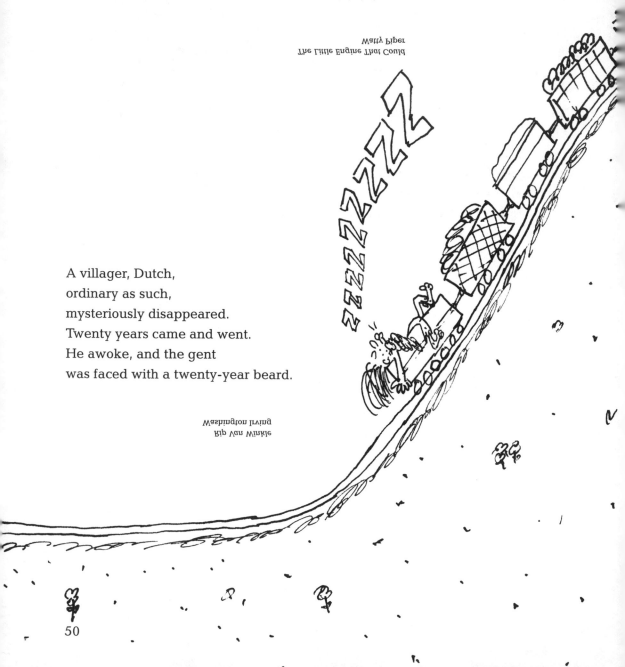

A villager, Dutch,
ordinary as such,
mysteriously disappeared.
Twenty years came and went.
He awoke, and the gent
was faced with a twenty-year beard.

Washington Irving
Rip Van Winkle

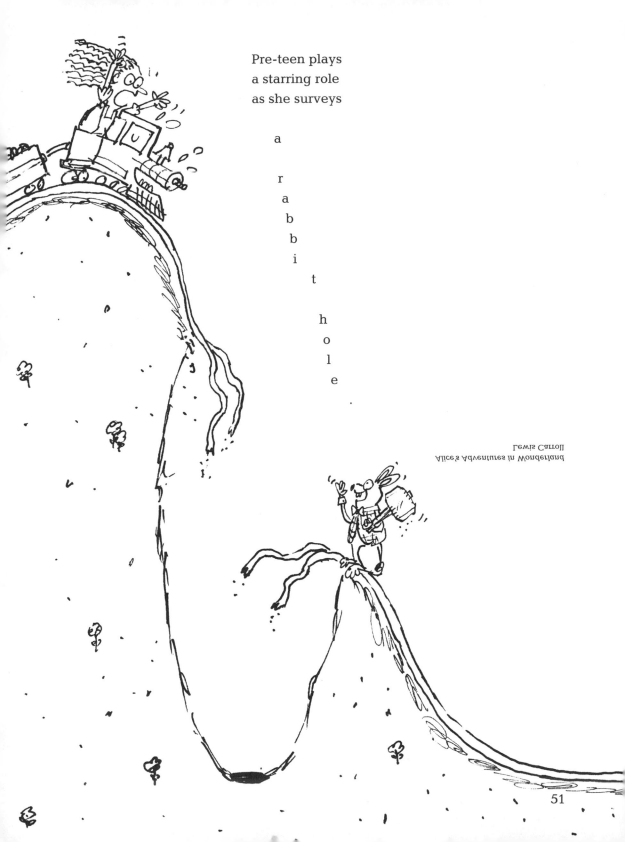

Pre-teen plays
a starring role
as she surveys

a

r
a
b
b
i
t

h
o
l
e

Alice's Adventures in Wonderland
Lewis Carroll

51

The Bear in the Kitchen

All I had was my peashooter
To scare off the bear intruder,
So I went on my computer,
Found a list of things to do:

—**Bears R Us Extermination.**
—**Call your local fire station!**
(When they sent me their dalmatian,
Ten-Spot didn't have a clue.)

—**Spray him with your carpet cleaner.**
—**Look, your average bear gets meaner**
  If he smells a turkey wiener.
Readers' comments? Even worse . . .

—**Try to broom-tickle his tummy.**
—**Got a stick of bubble gum? He**
  Will not chew it, the big dummy,
  But he'll hide it in your purse.

—**Bears (the brown ones) love dill pickle,**
  Ham and cheese on pumpernickel.
—**Did you know a red Popsicle**
  Makes him woozy? I could keep

Googling nonsense but because it
Sounds like thunder-snore, I pause it.
When I peek inside the closet . . .
Mr. Bear is fast asleep.

Tongue Twister
Trudy and Trina

Trudy Taylor tripped Trina Twoomey twice,
Twice Trina Twoomey tripped Trudy Taylor.
When Trina Twoomey tricked Trudy Taylor twice,
Trudy Taylor tried Trina Twoomey's trick.

Ha-ha-homonym

Sunny Sonny,
A minor miner
In a whole hole
Dug ore or
A few, *phew!*
Seams, it seems,
With hoes and hose
To load the lode,
Then shoot the chute,
And won one
Metal medal
Here, hear?

Universersagrams

Shooting star  Soars tonight!

Moon's light Night looms

Lunar eclipse Peculiar lens

Apollo landing site Spot in Galileo Land

Halley's Comet Yes, call me hot!

Asteroid It soared!

Streaks of lightning A night fork glistens

Sally K. Ride I'll dare sky

Lunar module A modern lulu

Large meteor Ore telegram

Crab Nebula Can be a blur

Neil Armstrong Normal gent, sir

The meteor shower The more, the worse

Whatever Happened to Oliver Tooke?

The plump-kins went on frowning,
The night was filled with gloom,
The witch rechecked her witch watch—
A minute half past doom—
And down the street came innocence,
Disguised as Captain Hook.
His name was Oliver Uriah Roy (O.U.R.) Tooke.

The witch was serving black ice scream.
She offered him a spoon.
When Captain Hook-Tooke took it,
He would swear he heard this tune:

I've lollipops
For Ollie-mops.
O.U.R. such a pest!
And poison pills
To give you chills
Till your untimely rest.

The night went black and blacker still
Than a black-hole-swallowed star.
The witch had taken Captain Hook
But who could guess how far?

She whisked him through the curtain fog
Upon a jiggery rake,
And where they flew nobody knew.
But, mates, make no mistake:
O.U.R. Tooke's been taken.
For upon the neighborhood
The horrifying echo fell,

"O.U.R.—gone for good!"

There Was a Cheetah

There was
a Cheetah,
Petey,
who met
a Puma,
Uma.
She was
a speedy,
yes indeedy,
meaty
kind
of cat.

That's why
the Cheetah
Petey
had asked
Miss Uma
Puma
to do
the fifty
in a swift
and nifty
nothing
flat.

What Does the J. Stand For?

When my Mother was calving
(I mean she was having
A pip of a boy—I was him!),
No one could agree
Whether baby should be
A Jackie, Jeff, Joey, or Jim.

"All we need's an initial
To make him official,"
Said Dad in the hospital ward.
He had pulled out his box
Of big alphabet blocks.
(My father gets easily bored.)

"Pick one!" Mother yelled,
As my father had spelled
Out a **J** with an **O**, **H**, **N**.
So he held up the **J**.
"That'll do," she would say,

And my Mother was right again.
See, the **J** is a proud
Letter. Shout it out loud,
"**J-J-J**." Now don't you feel better?
Other letters, like **X**,
Have the spunk one respects,
But the **J** is the smart baby's letter.

Mother said as she nursed me,
"Switch **J**. Put it first! He
Will love wearing it in the front."
That's how she laid claim
To the **J**. that became
The name of her own little runt.

Wacky Inventions

The Spider's Ladder

There was once a spider lover
Who said, "Science must discover
   How to set a spider free!"
And it is no laughing matter
Where he put a wooden ladder—
Now I pitter, potter, patter
   Up the tub A-S-A-P!

After walking on the water,
How I love to teeter-totter
   In the blue Jacuzzi skies.
Won't be getting any wetter,
As I knit a silky sweater,
And I'm feeling so much better
   Thanks to spider exercise!

A Leash for an Imaginary Pet

I have a dog who isn't there.
He isn't here or anywhere!
He doesn't come when he is called.
He has no fur. My dog is bald.
He never messes on the lawn.
He's what it means to say, "Doggone!"
The dog I have is rather weird.
He has completely disappeared.
And when I walk him, you should see
How oddly strangers look at ME!

Toilet Landing Lights

Bud stumbled in at three A.M.—
The middle of the night.
As usual he couldn't see
And couldn't find the light.
No need to worry though—Bud found
His seat upon the throne
Because the bowl lit up
Like something from the *Twilight Zone*.

Alexander Lion and P. Wee Mouse

After tea, cantaloupe,
And sautéed antelope,
Alexander arose from his chair
To enjoy shuffleboard
With a mouse, and he scored
As she landed just inside the square.

P. Wee said, *"Bravo, Alex"*—
(She squeaked in italics)—
"You hunk of a shuffleboard pro.
I, Magic Mouse Puck,
Am the model of pluck.
We belong in this shuffle floorshow."

Then they collared the Dogs,
And they butchered the Hogs.
The Chimpanzees should have stayed home.
How the crowd got a laugh
When bowlegged Giraffe
Flipped her puck overboard in the foam.

P. Wee shouted, *"Hooray!*
Coconuts and a lei
For the second-place Kangaroos."
Then with tears in his eyes,
Alex held up first prize,
A gold puck, the highlight of the cruise.

Forgetful

I went to school without my homework.
My teacher said, "That will not do."

The next day I forgot lunch money.
She said, "Is something wrong with you?"

The third day she was waiting for me.
"Did you bring everything, or not?"

"Oh, I remembered to remember.
I just forget what I forgot!"

When Billy Met Ginny

Buxton Elementary child,
Ginny Simpson, running wild
On the playground, saw her buddy,
Sammy Amadeo, bloody.
He'd been pushed and he was crying.
Billy Wodjekowski, trying
To be King of Everybody
(Kids were Billy's Silly Putty),
Said to Sammy, "Listen, skinny,
I'm the Boss . . ."

> *then he met Ginny!*

Tuna-on-a-Roll

I fishtail on the sand,
But sputter underwater.
I wish I were a grand
Amphibian hot-rodder.

I'm an arti-fish-al fish;
My license is invalid.
But this beats being someone's
Luncheon deli sub or salad.

Just steer clear of the ocean—
A drive-and-dive's no good.
To see this auto paddling
Is an unlikelihood.

Sunbathers understand
There's something fishy here.
A tuna should be canned,
Not driving down the pier.

The Frosty Feather

What all the world's been waiting for is here!
They've built a car that's lighter than the sky.
So grab your glasses, raise a toast—root beer,
And look—*The Frosty Feather.* It can fly!

But sadly the designer has an issue:
"People are much too heavy. Not allowed!
This beauty's made of misty wind and tissue,
Its paper engine runs on LIQUID CLOUD."

Marshmallow Fluff makes smooth and comfy seats.
The window cellophane prevents sun glare.
The fenders? Fog. Four doors? White cobweb sheets.
Airbags? Who needs an airbag in the air?

The lucky folks who ride *The Frosty Feather*
Must weigh about two ounces at the most.
The only question they ask you is whether
You qualify . . . climb in if you're a ghost.

Spotted Park Bench

I am a park bench.
Ordinary words cannot
express my thoughts on birds.

Tiger Stripes

Here's a fact they just found out:
A tiger's striped, both fur *and* skin!
But one small boy expressed a doubt.
He said, "May I take a look at him?"

Sammy Suspicious approached the cat,
"Kitty, what's this about striped *skin*
As well as fur?" The tiger sat,
Nodding, plotting, and said with a grin,

"My inside's like my skinside, kid,
Yellow prints for a jungle prince."
"Then open your mouth." The tiger did.
No one has seen Sammy since.

A Special Bond

Each time a child folds her hands,
She may be saying prayers for you,
Or else she just misunderstands
How to use the Elmer's glue.

Alphabet Weddings

About 250 identical twins have married identical twins in the world.

A twin,
Miss A,
of a twin,
Miss B,
weds a twin,
Mr. C,
of a twin,
Mr. D.

If twin D
marries B
when twin C
marries A,
it's officially
known as
a twin-stant
replay.

74

Mac Diddy

Computer Dog

Mac Diddy is a dog
Who writes a bitty blog
For anyone owning a pet.
You'll find on your browser
This miniature schnauzer
At dogwaggingtale.net.

M. Diddy's reviews
On Yorkies, shih tzus,
Pit bulls, Aussies, each breed of dog,
Make readers remark
That his bite and his bark
Are almost as good as his blog.

At Backward Elementary

At Backward Elementary School,
You get a topsy-turvy feeling.
Each May they crown the April Fool!
Custodians mop the ceiling.

The principal pea-shoots a note
To Mom, "Make sure your kid is late."
"For lunch"—he bangs the intercom—
"Throw out the pizza, eat the plate."

A teacher earns a falling star
By helping children fall asleep.
That's how to tell how bright they are:
They study math by counting sheep.

At Backward all the kids must spell
Drawkcab, of course, and uʍop ǝpᴉsdn,
And learn their grammar lessons well:
The verb goes underneath the noun.

At recess, teachers run and play.
In gym, the kids sit quietly.
Tomorrow? That was yesterday
At Backward Elementary.

It All Depends

The anger of an elephant
Depends upon the eleph-hunt.

The dinner of a honey bee
Depends on where the honey be.

The secret of a centipede
Depends upon its centi-speed.

The beauty of a platypus
Depends upon her platy-puss.

The safety of an antelope
Depends upon his ante-lope.

The future of a wildebeest
Depends upon a wilder beast.

The King Sees Himself in the Mirror

A King once wondered,
"Could there be
Not one but two
Of royal me?

"*Look there!* I see
My mirror kin,
My very own i-
dentical twin!"

And from his tower,
He shouted, "*Gee!*
There's two times more
Than one of me!"

The peasants cried,
"No, thank you, King.
What we want more
Than anything—

How can we make
This any clearer?—
Get rid of the birdbrain
In the mirror!"

Jump-Rope Rhyme

I got dressed up and went to school.
Hi and a hi and a hi-hi-hi
But it was summertime. April fool!
Ha and a ha and a ha-ha-ha

I went to the store with a shiny nickel.
Ho and a ho and a ho-ho-ho
I left the store with a nickel pickle.
Hey and a hey and a hey-hey-hey

I went to the trough to feed the pig.
Oink and an oink and an oink-oink-oink
The pig started dancing a piggety-jig!
Boink and a boink and a boink-boink-boink

I went to the movies and took my seat.
Woo and a woo and a woo-woo-woo
KING KONG WALKS DOWN SESAME STREET.
Oomp and an oomp and an oomp-oomp-oomp

I shook the cobwebs out of my head.
Ish and an ish and an ish-ish-ish
I turned out the light and I went to bed.
Shh and a shh and a shh-shh-shh

The moon swung down on a silvery beam.
Oh and an oh and an oh-oh-oh
I closed my eyes and I started to dream.
Ah and an ah and an ah-ah-ah

I dreamt I climbed the ladder of time.
Up and an up and an up-up-up
And that's the end of my jump-rope rhyme.
Bye and a bye and a good-bye-bye

Why Zebras Wear Stripes

Far out on the African plain,
Hyenas so often complain—
    An illegal blocker
    At Wildebeest Soccer!—
Which drives the hyenas insane.

Wild horses—the He's and the She's—
Do nothing but pick at their fleas.
    So the answer, of course, is
    To hire the horses,
Dressed up like they're referees.

Why Bears Love Bees

They're syruptitious.

Why Armadillos Wear Armor

An armadillo's like a rat but hairless
And that is why he wouldn't want to wear less,
Especially as it means people will stare less.

One silly 'dillo thought, "I'm quite a charmer,"
So he took off his heavy metal armor—
The cow fainted, two chickens, and the farmer!

Why Penguins Live in Antarctica

Their feet are made like water skis,
And skiing's easy minus knees.
(They're also filled with antifreeze.)

Grandpas Don't Know Everything

"There may be a monster in this house."
That's what my Grandpa said.

So to find out if maybe there *was* a monster
Hiding under my bed,
That's where I slid tonight's dinner—
Liver and onions—*ugh, the smell*!

Grandpa sniffed, then held his nose.
"That's a monster's dinner bell!"

Next morning, the liver and onions
With the napkin and napkin ring
Still stunk under my bed.

Grandpas don't know everything.

HaikUSA
City/State Riddles

My capital is
a car, a penny, and a
U.S. President.

NEBRASKA (Lincoln)

Only state with a
small stone right in the middle
for its capital

ARKANSAS (Little Rock)

In 1903
I was the first state to take
flight. Isn't that Wright?

NORTH CAROLINA

An anagram for
nominates contains the most
Scandinavians.

MINNESOTA

My legislature
has debateD over anD
over anD over.

DELAWARE (Dover)

From the nine letters
in my name, take away "ten"
and you're left with six.

TENNESSEE

Bugs' Mugs

I do believe
That butterflies
Are short vacations
For the eyes.

When caterpillars
Wiggle in,
I wait for music
To begin.

A dragonfly's
A hydroplane
With wonder wings
Of windowpane.

I even like
A spider's flair
For building bridges
In the air.

But when I see
A bug up close,
All I can say is
Adios!

The bug that looks
You in the face
Has just arrived . . .

From outer space!

Chills and Fever, Fever and Chills

You need a hug.
   You need a pill,
'Cause I'm the bug
   That made you ill.

I'm not a fly.
   I'm not a flea,
But I know why
   You've got a fe-

ver and a cold.
   I'm not a worm.
I'm not a mold.
   I am a germ,

So let's be clear:
   Just promise me
You won't go near
   A pharmacy!

Lady Bugmobile

Next to a flower hugged by a slug
Sits Freckles, Lady Buggy Bug,
   A garden rosemobile,
Who, idling on a thorny stem,
Crawls up a rose at twelve P.M.,
   Eyeing a drive-through meal.

Another Ladybug Bug sees
Freckles in a swarm of bees.
   Her name is Dot-to-Dot.
That single bug-powered engine Dodge
And Freckles land in a garage,
   Somewhere where bees are not.

Papa Bear

Papa is a morning bear—
Showers, pats his grizzly hair,
Throws his clothes on, scares the cat,
Shuffles down to breakfast. That
Closet is his hiding place—
Boo!—hugs Mama, rubs my face
With his whiskers, eats his grits,
Likes to growl before he sits
In his den to read the news,
Winks at me, unties his shoes;
Papa's ready for a snooze.

Can You Really Die of Boredom?

What a silly question!
If you're the one to ask it,
You've already got one
Foot in the casket.
Find out of the ordinary
Ways to behave,
Or life is going to be very . . .
Grave.

The Game of Love

IT's
One strokE of genius—
Set and match. Nothing is quite as
Exciting as enjoyiNg an exceptionaL
Rally at the baselIne, nonstop 'n' gO
Volleys, flaming Service aces, a loB
Easily half an iNch inside the line.
What a rackEt, what a fan's
fanTastic
game
of
l
o
v
e
!

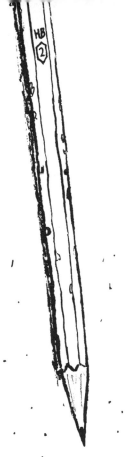

Corabelle and Mabel

As I sharpen my utensil—
Yellow No. 2 chewed pencil—
   Inspiration taps my brow.
I should write a little fable
About Corabelle and Mabel,
Who tells Cora, "If we're able,
   Why not chocolate-milk the cow?"

So I do, and here's the story,
Short but self-explanatory:
   From her udder point of view,
Mabel asks the cow, "Please, Jenny,
Give us chocolate milk aplenty?"
Says the cow, "If I had any . . .
   But I haven't anymoo!"

Cora gets the candy ready,
Mabel holds the bucket steady.
   "Jenny, will you swallow this?
It's not like the cud you're chewing."
Jenny knows what she is doing:
"To make chocolate milk" (she's mooing!),
   "I just ate a Hershey's Kiss!"

CHOCO CANDY   JENNY

CHOCO MILK! (BUCKET)   MABEL

CORA

93

Jimmy O'Flynn

Where will you sleep tonight, Jimmy O'Flynn,
The Over-and-Out or the Shut-eye Inn?

> *I'll fluff me a pillow here under the stars*
> *And capture the glitter in mayonnaise jars.*

Where are you going to, Jimmy O'Flynn?
Where could it be that you've never been?

> *Finding new places from the cradle to grave,*
> *I promised me mother that I would behave.*

Who will you take along, Jimmy O'Flynn,
A faraway neighbor or nearest of kin?

> *I'll take for companions a tipple of tea,*
> *A three-dollar bill, and a book on the sea.*

What are you looking for, Jimmy O'Flynn,
The upside down or the outside in?

> *There's only one mystery that matters to me—*
> *Is the future as far as they said it would be?*

Chrysalis

A magic spaceship
from earth to sky—
cuterpillar
       to beautifly.

Magician Definition

Magician: One who, for a laugh,
Saws his assistant clean in half,
Then makes an audience believe
That he has nothing up his sleeve.

Two Polliwogs

Metamorpho-
Sis and bro
Undergo strange
Frogettable change
And grow into co-
Owners of a bog
To keep up one wet dia-
L   O   G

The Loudest Snore

Kare Walkert
Sweden
93 decibels
May 24, 1993

His wife thought she would never hear
A sound to crush the human ear,
A sound she'd never heard before
Or since like his inhuman snore.

A motorbike? A fire hose?
A buffalo blowing his nose?
It sounded like a subway train
Pulled in the station of her brain!

How soon had she become aware
She'd married Mr. Grizzly Bear?
First night he went to sleep, she said,
He honked the pillows off the bed.

The Big Bang

Well, we thank you, Edwin Hubble,
That you took the time and trouble
To investigate just how the world began—

Like a universal splatter,
An exploding pupu platter,
A bazillion popcorn kernels in a pan.

How and why and when and whether
All that matter came together
Is a riddle not completely understood.

But there is a growing chorus—
Fifteen billion years before us,
Something definitely wrecked the neighborhood!

Mathemagical

There is a little thing I do
Whenever I feel bad.
I call the boys—
Subtract, Divide,
And Multiply and Add—
Four Horsemen of Arithmetic.
When I see them dismounting,
Those Great Corrections Officers
Have come to do my counting.

While Count Subtract falls somewhat shy
Of Addmiral's success,
Big Mr. Multiplenty grows,
But Sir Divide? By less.
Still, they cooperate to get
Me in the proper mood
To wield my pencil weaponry
Against the multitude.

When I can count on Multiply,
Divide, Subtract and Add,
It's something mathemagical,
And I don't feel so bad.

Giraffe Rap

After Gwendolyn Brooks

We be pinto. We
be neck. We
antenna. We
spot-check.

We be bone. We
be knee. We
be grown. We
be tree.

Olympic Dive

<u>I stride the ten-meter platform,</u>
abrupt cliff over-
looking the water
below. Trailing the
Russian champion
by two-tenths of
a point, I turn to
back-start a hawk-
fall. I leap, lean in,
touch toes, imitat-
ing the knife, no
wind, no splash,
no ripple—no end
to the scorecards
reading a perfect   !10!

Sand Speed Record

A Worm and a Snail
Ran a very grueling race.
You could tell by the sweat
On each one's face.
And they kept up
A nodder plodder
Millimeter pace
Till both of them tied
For first last place.

Dragon Dinner Etiquette

Approved Dragon drinks:
Boys-in-berry Juice,
Injure Ale,
Cough-ee.

Do not accept a dinner invitation
If St. George is the guest of honor.

When eating Chinese food,
Use chop stakes.

If you've ordered pizza instead,
Spare the delivery boy.

Do not tell the waiter your food is undercooked.
Flame broil it yourself.

When blowing your nose at the table,
Use a bedspread.

If the dragon sitting next to you burps,
Applaud.

For dessert, order Cookie Monsters.

After-Dinner Rule:
Never ask for a doggie bag.

One-Worders

Adolescent Time-Out: Quaranteen

Sore Loser's Best Wishes: Congrudgulations

Escape Hatch: Troublechute

The Donkey Brothers

They had a grueling tug-of-war,
A donkey and his brother.
They pulled and pulled and pulled some more,
First one way, then the other.

Back and forth they went until
One would be the boss.
The moral is that donkeys should
Not share their dental floss.

Farmer Herbie

Farmer Herbie milked the cow
Once his daughter taught him how.

Farmer Herbie milked the bull—
He got creamed upside his skull.

Herbie's still a dairy farmer,
Farming in a suit of armor.

The Case of the Missing Smile

A boy who wished to play at spies
Was fortunate to have three eyes.
The third eye, in a paper sack,
He took out just to watch his back.

He met a girl who was renowned
For opening a Lost-and-Found,
A-Sly-Whodunit-I-Spy Ring,
And she could find most anything.

So these two agents took the case—
THE GIRL WHOSE SMILE ESCAPED HER FACE
(THE GRIN THAT SUDDENLY SKIPPED TOWN).
Now all the girl could do was frown.

They measured teeth and lips and gums.
(Her mouth was full of cookie crumbs.)
They secretly collected files
On what would bring a thousand smiles:

A book—*Lost Grins and Where They Went*,
The recipe for merriment,
A tickle backscratcher, and yes,
Two buckets full of nuttiness.

Her smile returned, and what a face!
But now the girl has one more case
The spies are busy working on—
Poor thing, her two front teeth are gone!

Limb-ericks

The Leg

On the shore of an African river,
There's a sleeping Flamingo aquiver.
    You can't help but think
    She's so pretty in pink,
But the crocodile's thinking chopped liver.

The Wing

The Condor, though peaceful asleep,
Has a wingspan the length of a Jeep,
    And those keen rifle eyes
    Spot a thousand horseflies
Making pigs of themselves on a sheep.

The Elbow

The point of these joints, if you please
(Skin-and-boney parentheses),
    Should remind you you're not
    The great beauty you thought:
They're as wrinkled and knobby as knees.

Limericks

Australian Hop

A Kangaroo mother named Chloe
Wears a "Baby Aboard" sign to show he,
   Tucked safely inside,
   Gets a cushioned 'roo ride—
That luggage of huggage named Joey.

Blue and Green Eyes

A Peacock's the bird Dapper Dan.
He's a he-man of Pakistan.
   Though the Peahen gets wise,
   She's a fan in his eyes
All because of the "eyes" in his fan.

The Beak

The rain forest sheltered a cute place
For a Toucan who looked like a fruit-face.
   But across the cabana,
   They knew that banana
Was simply a mouthful of suitcase!

Wizard of Alakazam

I'm the Elementary Wizard
Of PS 82.
You won't believe the wild-child,
Wizardy things I do.

I pull blue scarves from evening
And wrap them around midnight.
I double-knot six moonbeams
To dizzy the world with light.

If you get stuck in yesterday,
Tell me—I'll set you free.
You cannot skip tomorrow
Unless you skip with me.

Pretend you're a sea captain
And this is your last cruise:
We'll sail the ocean pinks and reds
Instead of greens and blues

Around Cape of Good Morning
By SS *Coffee Cup*.
And I might be a Wizard even
After I wake up.

Alphabet Riddles: Five Poems

Navigate through the alphabet—
You will not see a one-letter pet.
But can you find a flying pair
Of one-letter animals in the air?

B and J = bee and jay

I start with E,
I end with E.
Forward or backward,
I'm still me,
And in between,
I'm two times V.

W = V ewe—two times V = A

On the far end is M,
On the near end is M,
And O how it touches
The two of them.

MOM

You see this once in every hour
And in a split second,
But not in a minute.
It happens twice in two months,
But not in a week,
And never in an entire year.

The letter O

It starts with H
and ends with S.
Now see if you can spot
in between this creature's name
the most gigantic pot!

Hippopotamus

Too Fast, I'm Afraid

Timmy McAllister, 9, was afraid
Of whatever moved faster than him.
He wanted a pet—a dog or a cat—
But nope, they moved faster than Tim.

So his parents decided to buy him a turtle.
That pokey turtle was also 9.
The turtle went everywhere Timmy would go,
Slower
And slower
And slower
Than slow,
Following Timmy in line.

They partied at birthdays when they were just 10.
Then 20,
Then 50,
Then 80!
That pair,
A man and his turtle, grew older than old,
But neither of them seemed to care.

And here they are now at 105—
Congrats to the turtle and Tim!
But Timmy's afraid because most of the time
The turtle moves faster than him.

The Book Booth

There's not a big selection,
It's not locked for protection,
But at the intersection
Of Booth and Telephone,

Two customers politely
Can snuggle in it (tightly)
And go once over (lightly)
The books they'd like to own.

"Readcycle" means you leave one—
A book you love. Retrieve one . . .
Who knows? You might receive one
You haven't read before.

Hats off to the committee
For such an itty-bitty
Library in the city,
Which proves that less is more.

Miniver Mouse

Miniver Mouse, a thief of cheese,
   Grew fur and fat
   On Swiss and cheddar:
He lived a rodent's life of ease
   And none was better.

Miniver loved a cheese fondue,
   A block of brick,
   A slice of Edam.
He gained another chin or two
   And lost his freedom.

Miniver cried, "Oh, let me in!
   I'm much too fat
   To squeeze through plumbing.
If only I could *wish* me thin—
   But look who's coming!"

His mouse mates took their axes out
   And whacked the hole—
   (The Cat was creeping!)—
A nifty trick they'd read about
   In *Good Mousekeeping*.

The Universal Turtle Verse

I spend the day nibbling rent-free
Underneath the *Giving Tree.*
Me, Rirty Dat and Snerry Jake
Show Runny Babbit how to make
Up verses. Then I lug my hump
(Careful not to bump the Glump)
Into the woods to trade a word
With the argle-bargle bird:
Nuthatch wisely recommends,
Find out where the sidewalk ends.

SHELL SILVERSTEIN

Your Monkey's Uncle

He calls you on the telephone.
His voice sounds like the dial tone
Until it *SQUEAKS*! A saxophone?
   Who's there? Your Monkey's Uncle.

He says, "I'm coming over soon."
You say, "But we'll be gone till June!"
Because he's such a loony tune,
   That nut, your Monkey's Uncle.

Is that him on the fire escape?
He uses it to stay in shape,
A fitness chimp who's going ape,
   Your hunky Monkey's Uncle.

Turn off the lights and lock the lock
Because no one can stand the shock
Of seeing . . . *Wait*, was that a knock?
   He's here! Your Monkey's Uncle.

Wiped Out

On every playground,
there's lots of dirt.

You don't believe me?
Ask your shirt.

Dude Food

Get my brussels sprouts in Brussels.
All my pastries should be Danish.
Make my sausages Vienna.
Giant lobsters? Mainly Maine-ish.

Ship my baked beans in from Boston.
Cream cheese ought to come from Philly.
Ham has got to be Virginia.
Spicy hot? It's Texas Chili.

Oranges? Pick them fresh in Florida.
Peaches? From the Georgia border.
Pineapples must be Hawaiian.
Dude food's always made to order.

Avocado
The Magic Fruit

Run over
an avocado
with your auto . . .

And by gosh,
summer squash.

Honk If You're a Reader!

In the back of our Toyota,
I am sitting sipping soda,
Reading something good like *Harriet the Spy*.
Mom is driving—she's a speeder—
You should honk if you're a reader.
That's the only way she'll ever let you by.

Someone's shouting, *"Watch it, lady!"*
We are doing nearly eighty
When she sees the kid with *Where the Wild Things Are*,
And his dad is honking—*madly!*
So my mother waves and gladly
Lets the angry driver in the other car

Pass us, even though he's sneering.
Then he's laughing while he's steering
For it slowly dawns on him just what it takes:
Oh, the only way to beat her
Is to honk if you're a reader
So she'll smile at you and quickly tap the brakes.

The 100ᵗʰ Day

The principal dressed as Elvis
And sang to a twang guitar.
The janitor came as a pickle
And smelled like a vinegar jar.
My teacher got his head shaved
And, covered with Reddi-wip,
He looked like a six-foot cupcake
Till the whipped cream started to drip.

The kids got three-hour recess.
School lunch was two hours more.
Homework assignments? Canceled.
Each kid got a perfect score.
The hundredth day was an excellent day—
Not the day before
Or the very next day—
But the hundredth?
That was the greatest day
That anyone ever knew.
I guess I should mention one sad fact:
I was at home with the flu.

A Girl I Really Liked A Lot

A girl I really liked a lot
    Came up to me in school
And gave me this sweet Valentine
    Card for April Fool.

Baseball-o-grams

Shoestring catch  Gosh, I can stretch!

World Series seats? Seats were sold, sir.

No-hitter Then riot

Stolen base Noble asset

Outfield Flied out Fouled it

Called third strike Thrill sidetracked

Spitball Lip blast

Star's autograph Grasps at author

Relief pitcher Help, rectifier

Ladies' Day Lady's idea?

Crowding the plate Hitter glanced . . . *pow!*

Satchel Paige Pitches a gale

Manager Ran game

Yankees lead! Seek any deal

Most Valuable Player Marvel, Pa, absolutely

Double play Yep, dual lob!

Oh, c'mon, happiness is a . . . Championship season

We Played in a Soup Tureen

I was a stalk of asparagus,
And Al was a butter bean,
And Sal was the head of a cauliflower.
We played in a soup tureen.

Then Sal was a slice of cinnamon toast,
And Al was juice in a jar,
And I was a buttery substitute.
We ran a breakfast bar.

Then Al was a cup and a half of flour,
And I was a leg and a thigh,
And Sal was the broth and the salt in the broth.
We stewed in a chicken pot pie.

When sister Sal was a buffalo snort,
Bro Al was a restless mule,
And I was the seven o'clock alarm—
It was time to get dressed for school.

Bigfoot's Big Feet

I am the modern-day Neanderthal.
Where can I find a classy sassy shoe?
I spent the day shopping at Big 'N' Tall—
Why don't they carry my size—62?
Can you imagine how a giant feels
Whose only claim to fame is that he's known
As being one of nature's biggest heels?
No wonder I spend all my time alone.
But I'll come out of hiding in the woods
And put my best foot forward just to meet
Someone who'd share a few consumer goods.
Flip-flops? Now that would be a major feat.

The Knuckleheaded Scientist

A knuckleheaded scientist
Had got his knickers in a twist.
 "The dinosaur
 Is such a bore,"
He said. "I've found what others missed."

"*They never lived!*" proclaimed the sleuth
Triumphantly. "And that's the truth!"
 But that was odd
 Because the clod
Was sitting on a . . .
 giant tooth!

Epitaphs

For a Parrot

Listen. Do you hear that sound?
Like someone's nonstop squawking!
It's coming from beneath the ground . . .
I WASN'T FINISHED TALKING!

For a Camel

The only animal underground
with a cool dual burial mound.

For a Rat

She finally found
A pet-friendly
Anacondo

For a Vulture

He picked at warthog, pecked at stork,
Poked at lion, packed in pork,
Got so fat on tubs of germs . . .
Now he's facing grubs and worms.

For an Opossum

Here lies the body
of a shy opossum,
who wishes you hadn't
run across him.

Ripton Claude, NYPD

Ripton Claude (a.k.a. Ripped 'n' Clawed) is a Rottweiler K-9 dog.

I am in charge of **THEFT & FRAUD**,
  I prowl each city street.
My name? Inspector Ripton Claude,
81st Detective Squad—
  Manhattan is my beat.

The fashionably dashing Dog,
  Preposterously smashing Dog,
    The swashbuckling and slashing Dog,
      Rip Claude, NYPD

That burglar, Cat-Ten-Lives-Or-More,
  Was up to deeds most foul.
She sneaked in Kuddly Kitten's store
And stole the catnip cats adore,
  But I was on the growl.

Cat wasn't at the Waldorf,
She wasn't at the Ritz.
She wasn't playing dominoes
With Ape Abramowitz.

She wasn't on the subway
Or the Staten Island Ferry.
She wasn't in the New York
City Kitty Cemetery.

Cat wasn't in the county morgue
Or in intensive care.
I checked her hair salon,
Curl Up 'n' Dye. She wasn't there.

But Ripton Claude knew what to do.
I knew just where she'd be—
Catnapping on Fifth Avenue,
And that's where she surrendered to
Police Rottweiler, me . . .

The fashionably dashing Dog,
Preposterously smashing Dog,
The swashbuckling and slashing Dog,
Rip Claude, NYPD

The Gulper Eel

When your gigantic head turns sharply into tail—
I see the joker in the evolutionary scale.

But here's a mouth manipulated by a hinge—
The python of the ocean deep—to make its victims cringe.

In blackness far beyond the continental shelf,
Your sack-gullet devours prey much larger than yourself,

Six feet in length—and more it seems in ghostly breadth.
I realize to lure fish, first, you scare them half to death.

The Ghost Slug

You might just think a slug's a slug,
But this bad boy will chug-a-lug
Earthworms as soon as it gets dark.
A subterranean great white shark,
He has no color, has no eyes,
Nothing but a pale disguise.
You'd know he's nasty as he seems
If you could hear the earthworm screams.

Elsewhere in the Universe

If the sun were lemon Jell-O,
And the moon Limburger cheese,
And all the clouds were yellow-
Green volleyballs of breeze;
If the seas were low-fat yogurt,
And the islands loaves of bread,
If forests did not push up trees
But Chia Pets instead;
If you were a chocolate mustache,
And I were a peanut-butter purse,
Then we would be living somewhere
Else in the universe.

Surprise: Three More Book Riddles

To prove you are a princess,
though it may sound absurd,
try sleeping on a mountain
of mattresses. I've heard
only a *real* princess
will toss and turn her head
all night if there's one tiny
vegetable in her bed.

Hans Christian Andersen
The Princess and the Pea

Now one toy tells another
It won't be just a toy
If, rescued from the toy box,
It's treasured by a boy.

One day the boy who loves the toy
Falls ill, then moves away.
The boy's wish is forbidden;
Sadly, the toy must stay.

There's magic in the *real* tear
The toy weeps for the child—
It brings the Nursery Fairy
Who leads it to the wild.

Margery Williams
The Velveteen Rabbit

A chimney is
this EVEning's door
for presents you
were hoping for.

Clement Clarke Moore
"'Twas the Night Before Christmas"

I'm the Library Lady

If you're looking for good fiction,
Welcome to my jurisdiction
   In the Dewey Decimal yard.
I can find the perfect story,
Humor (goofy), vampire (gory),
Novels (grand), adventure (glory) . . .
   Let me see your library card.

No, there's nothing more exciting
For someone who's into writing
   Than to fricassee a mind,
'Cause a book is like an oven—
What it's cookin' is book lovin'.
Set the temperature, then shove in
   Every brain cell you can find.

Notes Left Behind on the Blackboard

Whenever I hear teachers mention
My name it's followed by "detention."

My going-away present
is in your desk, Mrs. Trout...
unless it already crawled out.

The principal is my best friend,
Okay?
His office corner's where I spend
The day.

Teachers like homework just because

They love encyclopedias.

145

Close Encounters of . . .

The *first* kind:
When you see a UFO at close range,
Say you're standing on your roof.

The *second* kind:
When you see a UFO, and you have
Photographic proof.

The *third* kind:
When you see an extraterrestrial (ET),
If only for a minute.

The *fourth* kind:
When the UFO takes off . . .
with you in it!

The *fifth* kind:
Never mind.

Bananappeal?

I wish bananas just came plain
Without a long mushy membrane,
That nauseating food chain chain.

If I so much as *see* a string,
I tweezer off the ugly thing
As gummy as a bathtub ring.

Would you eat hot dogs wearing hair?
No! Say good-bye to a fruit's nightmare.
Who likes banana underwear?

Nicknames in the NBA
A Found Poem

Big Ticket, Big Country, Big Baby,
Z, Zo, Rip, Bo, Tip, Mo, Pip, Lo, Stro,
Cat, Doggie, Piggie, Goat, Snake, Bull, Horse.
Sam I Am, Tim Bug, Tin Man, Thunder Dan,
Sir Dunks-A-Lot, Boom Dizzle, The Hobbit,
Vinsanity, Mt. Motumbo, White Chocolate,
Vanilla Gorilla, Dollar Bill, Tractor, Scooter,
Ukraine Train, The Owl Without a Vowel,
The Human Highlight Film, Durantula,
Magic, Shaq, Larry Legend, The Chosen One,
His Airness.

Lindy Hopper

A girl named Lindy Hopper,
Who can really dance a jig,
Can also tell a whopper
Bigger than, well,

. . . VERY BIG.

Whenever Lindy H. starts dancing,
Out will pop a whopper:
Like "I do graceful swan dives"
(Every one's a belly-flopper).
She owns a "Shetland pony"
(It's a sheltie/cockapoo).
She once piloted an ocean liner
(Built like a canoe).
"Mayonnaise on cauliflower"
Is what she feeds her cat.
She said she found a brand-new bug
(But we call it a gnat).
She's traveled all around the world
So often she's lost count,
And climbed a "little foothill" (twice!)
Called Everest (as in *Mount*).
She helicoptered to the moon
(And that was in bad weather!),
Then faster than the speed of light,
Flew back by pigeon feather.
So if you meet Miss Lindy "Whopper"
Hopper, you'll conclude
She makes her watchers watch her dance
And keeps her listeners glued.

149

Having Escaped from the Sandy Eggo Zoo,
The Tiger and the Monkey Get Married

Six shiny Turtle bridesmaids wore
Six toilet-paper veils.
A Pelican, the best man, nudged
Six mushy usher Snails.

The Tiger wore his Tiger tux
And cummerbund, the rogue.
The Monkey's gown? A tea cozy
She'd read about in *Vogue*.

She rose on splendid tender paws,
Glittering in the sun,
And twirled to monkey waltzes
With her Tiger No. 1.

A Rabbit was the Rabbi
(If you take away the "t")
For weddings are exactly where
A Rabbi ought to be.

"A raisin toast," the Rabbi said,
"To Abigail, the bride,
And blushing Tiger-hearted
Ebenezer by her side,"

Which cheered and charmed the islands.
Easy winds were setting sail,
And so were magic sea songs
Whistled by the Prince of Whale.

When Ebenezer roared, the Monkey
Howled, and you just knew,
Two sounds were never sweeter
Than "I DO!" and then "ME, TOO!"—
About 4,000 miles from
The Sandy Eggo Zoo.

The Arm-y Navy

To an octopus luncheon for nine,
These comrades-in-arms come to dine.
 But when hugging each other—
 What suckers, oh brother!—
They look like a great ball of twine.

In Short

In Baltimore, an Oriole—
In short, a Baltimoriole—
Was looking most arboreal
(In short, up in a tree).

An Earthworm territorial—
In short, a Wormemorial
To dirt—was most pictorial
(In short, the worm was me).

A lesson Baltimoriole—
In short, his bird tutorial—
Would leave this Wormemorial
Too short. . . .

Gratitude

It began when
Froggy's muffle
turned to piffle,
then *tap-tap!*
Toad did not
want a kerfuffle
with a Frog
to stop his nap.
But Frog's sniffle
was no bluffle—
he was waiting
for the log.
Toadie still
refused to scuffle
as he watched
a polliwog.
He would not
play second fiddle
to this riddle
of a Newt,
but he hopped
across the middle
just a little
for the brute.
So they sat there
all day glaring,
staring at the
riverbanks.
Late at night,
across the foggy
boggy, Froggy
whispered, **"Thanks."**

The Impossibles

You cannot seed a garden
With wheelbarrows of dreams.
Unless you first plant wishes, how
Cucumbersome it seems.

You cannot climb a rainbow
Unless the winds agree
To blow in one direction—up—
Toward Curiosity.

You cannot live in castles
Suspended in the air,
But your imagination takes
Long vacations there.

You cannot reach Forever—
Forever's much too far—
But fortunately Now and Then
Were built right where you are.

You cannot catch Tomorrow
Until you catch your sleep.
Can you recall how many Yes-
terdays you wish to keep?

You cannot snatch Sir Shadow—
He's such a clever chap!
Until—at night—he snatches *you*
And dozes in your lap.

157

Index of Titles